# Airplanes

## Mary Kate Doman

### Enslow Elementary

an imprint of

### Enslow Publishers, Inc.

40 Industrial Road
Box 398
Berkeley Heights, NJ 07922
USA

http://www.enslow.com

*For Liam, who loves things that go*

Enslow Elementary, an imprint of Enslow Publishers, Inc.

Enslow Elementary® is a registered trademark of Enslow Publishers, Inc.

Copyright © 2012 by Enslow Publishers, Inc.

All rights reserved.

No part of this book may be reproduced by any means
without the written permission of the publisher.

**Library of Congress Cataloging-in-Publication Data**

Doman, Mary Kate.
 Airplanes / by Mary Kate Doman.
   p. cm. — (All about big machines)
 Summary: "Learn how airplanes are used every day"— Provided by publisher.
 Includes bibliographical references and index.
 ISBN 978-0-7660-3933-9
 1. Airplanes—Juvenile literature. I. Title.
 TL547.D66 2012
 629.133'34—dc23
                                                2011014533

Paperback ISBN 978-1-59845-240-2

Printed in the United States of America

**To Our Readers:** We have done our best to make sure all Internet Addresses in this book were active and appropriate when we went to press. However, the author and the publisher have no control over and assume no liability for the material available on those Internet sites or on other Web sites they may link to. Any comments or suggestions can be sent by e-mail to comments@enslow.com or to the address on the back cover.

♻ Enslow Publishers, Inc., is committed to printing our books on recycled paper. The paper in every book contains 10% to 30% post-consumer waste (PCW). The cover board on the outside of each book contains 100% PCW. Our goal is to do our part to help young people and the environment too!

**Photo Credits:** © 2011 Photos.com, a division of Getty Images. All rights reserved, pp. 10–11, 16–17, 18–19, 23; David Meintel/Shutterstock.com, p. 20; Fernando Blanco Calzada/Shutterstock.com, p. 2 (title page); ID1974/Shutterstock.com, pp. 4–5; Pincasso/Shutterstock.com, pp. 8–9; Shutterstock.com, pp. 14–15; UNGOR/Shutterstock.com, pp. 6–7; Vacclav/Shutterstock.com, pp. 12–13.

**Cover Photo:** David Meintel /Shutterstock.com

# Note to Parents and Teachers
Help pre-readers get a jumpstart on reading. These lively stories introduce simple concepts with repetition of words and short simple sentences. Photos and illustrations fill the pages with color and effectively enhance the text. Free Educator Guides are available for this series at www.enslow.com. Search for the *All About Big Machines* series name.

# Contents

# Words to Know

**airplane**    **clouds**    **people**

# There are many kinds of airplanes.

# All are fun to see.

# Some take off on land.

# Some land at sea.

# They pick people up.

They drop people off.

# Airplanes fly near.

# Airplanes fly far.

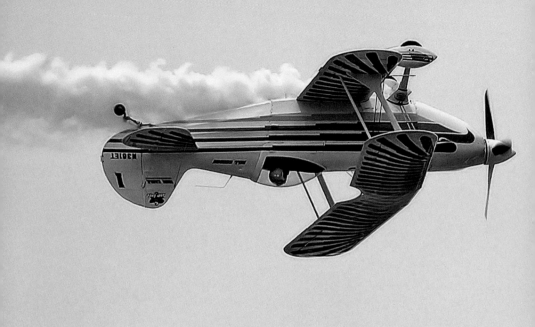

Sometimes airplanes go round and round and upside down.

They are so many
kinds of airplanes!

# Read More

Kirk, Ellen. *My Plane Book*. New York: HarperCollins, 2006.

Millard, Anne. *Big Book of Airplanes*. New York: Dorling Kindersley Publishing, 2001.

Mitton, Tony. *Amazing Airplanes*. London: Kingfisher, 2005.

# Web Sites

*Airplanes for Kids*
<http://www.airplanesforkids.com>

*The Museum of Flight*
<http://www.museumofflight.org/>

# Index

Guided Reading Level: C
Guided Reading Leveling System is based on the guidelines recommended by Fountas and Pinnell.

Word Count: 50